Puns are the perfect mix of wordplay, humor, and a little bit of groaning. They've been around for thousands of years, from ancient texts to today's memes, and they're all about playing with words that sound alike or have double meanings.

But what exactly makes them so irresistible?

Language Quirks

Puns thrive on homophones (words that sound the same but mean different things) and homonyms (words with multiple meanings), which makes language a playground for punsters.

Our Love for Double Meanings

Puns surprise us. That "aha!" moment when a word takes on a new meaning is what makes them so satisfying—and often hilarious.

Historical Roots

Puns aren't new! They've been used in ancient Egyptian texts, Greek plays, and even Shakespeare's works, where he dropped over 3,000 puns.

Brain Wiring

Our brains are wired to spot patterns and make connections, so puns exploit that tendency, giving us a little twist that keeps us on our toes.

Puns are born from language's quirks and our brain's love for cleverness—a timeless recipe for laughter.

SCOTT MATTHEWS

The Big Book of Puns

202 Silly Puns, Clever Jokes and Wordplay

Ready to dive deeper into the world of puns?

Why did the cookie cry? Because his father was a wafer so long!

I used to work in a shoe recycling shop. It was sole-destroying.

There's a new type of broom out: it's sweeping the nation.

Whiteboards are remarkable.

I took a vacation
in the Arctic.
Cool trip.

I wanted to be a history teacher...
But there's no future in it.

I accidentally glued myself
to my autobiography.
That's my story, and I'm sticking to it.
MY LIFE

I met a skeleton
at a party.
He had no body to
dance with.

My friend wants to become
an archaeologist,
but life's just too much of a dig right now.

My plane joke
didn't land.

What do you call an
alligator in a vest?
An investigator.

Why are cats so good at video games?
Because they have nine lives.
REVIVE?

I told my curtains we needed space.
They drew themselves shut.

What do cows tell each other
at bedtime?
Dairy tales.

Why do bees have sticky hair?
Because they use honeycombs.

Why did the grape stop in the middle of the road?
It ran out of juice.
REST AREA

I dated someone from
the library.
We had too many issues.
OVERDUE

I tried to start a hot sauce company,
but I couldn't handle the heat.
HOT SAUCE

I named my dog "Coffee" because he always grounds me.

Want to hear a pizza joke?
Never mind, it's too cheesy.

I once dated an artist,
but he just painted me in a bad light.

I lost my remote.
Now everything's out
of control.

I ordered a chicken and an egg.
I'll let you know what comes first.

LAUNCH SITE
I wanted to be an astronaut,
but my career never took off.

I wanted to be a historian,
but I just couldn't get
past the present.
HISTORY
HISTORY
HISTORY
HISTORY
HISTORY
PRESENT DAY
HISTORY

What's a pirate's
favorite subject?
Arrrrt.

TIME TRAVEL AVAILABLE
DINO
TOUR
I walked into a travel agency
and asked about time travel.
They said, "You're early."

Why didn't the lion win the race?
Because he was racing a cheetah.
FINISH

The stapler is the most well-attached office supply.

The scissors and I
had a falling out.
Things got a
bit snippy.

I don't trust stairs.
They're always up to something.

I once had a job as a
human statue,
but I just couldn't stand it.

BANK
I quit my job
as a banker;
it just didn't
make cents.

Why did the octopus beat the shark in a fight?
Because it was well armed.

The elevator business has its ups and downs.

What did one hat say to the other?

Stay here, I'm going on ahead.

I dated a locksmith once.
She had the key to my heart.

I drove my car into
a tree yesterday.
Now I'm really stumped.

I'd tell you a joke about trains,
but it might go off the rails.
JOKE BOOK

I tried to eat
a clock.
It was time-consuming.

I tried writing with a broken pencil...
But it was pointless.

I once ate a dictionary.

It gave me thesaurus throat ever.

I just burned 2,000 calories.
I forgot the pizza in the oven.

THINK OUTSIDE THE BOX
Claustrophobic people are more productive thinking outside the box.

What do you call a
cow with no legs?
Ground beef.

I wrote a song about tortillas...

But it's a little flat.

Do you know sign language?
You should learn it: it's pretty handy.

What do you call a sheep covered in chocolate?
A candy baa.

The accountant broke up with his calculator.

He felt like he was just another number.

I saw a
chicken
at the gym.
It was working
on its pecks.

I bought a ladder.
It's a step up in life.

I got promoted to head of staplers.
It was a binding decision.
HEAD OF STAPL

CAMOUFLAGE PANTS
?
I bought camouflage pants,
but I can't find them.

The math teacher called me obtuse.
I said, "That's not right."

BUSINESS
CEO-YO
I started a company
making yoyos...
It has its ups and downs.

My cat was
just sick on
the carpet,
I don't think
it's feline well.

My mirror got dramatic.
Now it's reflecting on everything.

What do you call a group of musical whales?
An orca-stra.

I went to Egypt,
but it was all just
a pyramid scheme.

I told my plants I love them.
Now I'm rooted in commitment.

I built a model of Mount Everest.
It's a high point in my life.

O
Au
The periodic table's parties are pretty elementary.

I adopted a snail. We're bonding, but it's taking things slow.
DAY 30: STILL MOVING IN.

I made a belt out
of sausages.
It was a waist of meat.

I tried working at a
blanket factory,
but I got covered in work.

My job at the calendar factory was short-lived.
I took a few days off.
MISSING

The moon threw a party, but no one came.
Guess it needed more space.

Why did the student bring a
ladder to class?
To go to high school.

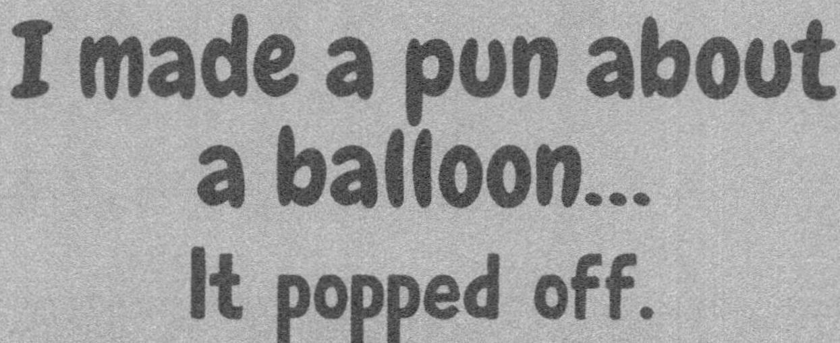

I made a pun about
a balloon...
It popped off.

How do you organize an
outer space party?
You planet.

I broke up with my fridge.
It was too cold.

MONTH
I had abs once.
Now they're just...
ab-sent.

I told my date she had a
great sense of direction.
She left.
EXIT

I was gonna end this list with a joke about paper,
joke about paper,
but it's tearable.

That peanut
butter was
so good.
It was nuts.
PEANUT
BUTTER

My washing machine ghosted me.
It just stopped spinning me around.

I work at a paper factory.
It's a real sheet show.

I quit my janitor job.
The job was sweeping me away.

Do you know where you can get chicken broth in bulk?
The stock market.
BROTH ↑
BROTH
BROTH

I named my printer
Bob Marley,
because it's always jammin'.

I got hired at a shoelace company.
I'm tied up at the moment.

I opened a GPS company.
I needed some direction in life.
N
W
E
S

Why did the student bring a flashlight to class?
flashlight to class?
To brighten their future.

I dated a candle once.
It burned out.

I bought a cloak of invisibility.
I can't find it now.

I told a joke about unemployment,
but it never worked.

I tried to sell my vacuum,
but it sucked too much to keep.

I used to sell bonsai trees.
It was my "small business."
SHOP

What's the difference between a well-dressed man on a bicycle and a badly dressed man on a tricycle? Attire.

I started a memory club...
But we keep forgetting to meet.
MEETING TODAY?

I don't know what happened
to my imaginary friend.
He ghosted me.

I tried to make a pun
about infinity....
But it never ends.

√root
I put my root beer in a
square cup.
Now it's just beer.

I put my phone in
airplane mode.
It took off without me.

It was an emotional wedding.
Even the cake had tiers.

Why did the dog sit
in the shade?
Because it didn't want to be a hot dog.

One bird can't make a pun.
But toucan.

I started talking to my blender.

It really mixed things up.

MAPS
ARE
PUNNY
I made a pun about maps,
but it didn't go anywhere.

My math teacher
called me average.
How mean!
MEAN
MEDIAN
AVERAGE

The stars started a union.
They were tired of working night shifts.

Did you hear about the guy who lost the left side of his body?

He's alright now.

The elevator and I have a
complicated relationship;
it always lets me down.
OUT
ORDER

The Moon broke up
with Earth;
it said it needed space.

The microwave started
dating the toaster,
talk about a heated relationship.

I got hired at the zoo.
The pay is bananas.

I sell speakers.
Business is booming.
BOOM!
BOOM!

I didn't realize I bought a broken fan.
It was a huge blow.

I'm reading a horror novel in Braille.
Something bad is going to happen...
I can feel it.

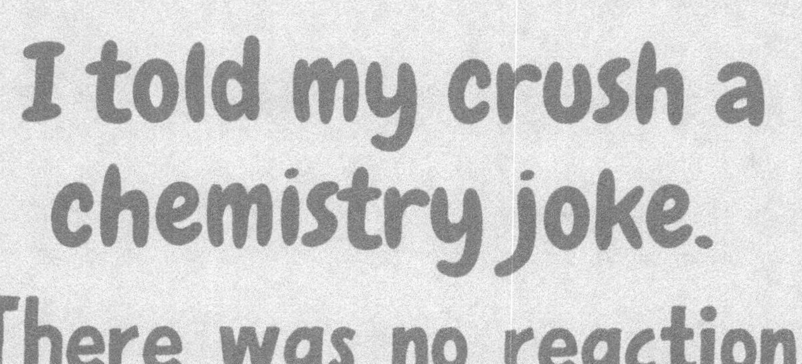
I told my crush a chemistry joke.
There was no reaction.

EXPERIMENT:
LOVE
POTION #0

Why can't
leopards hide?
They're always spotted.

I'm reading a book about anti-gravity. It's impossible to put down!

I wanted to study archaeology, but my career's in ruins.
RESUME

Just call
me Fsh.
What do you call a fish
with no eyes?
Fsh.

I went on a once-in-a-lifetime trip.

Never again.

Why don't scientists trust atoms?
Because they make up everything!
ATOMIC BEHAVIOR REPORT
TRUST ISSUES?
WE MADE IT ALL!

I used to be a baker,
but I couldn't make enough dough.

What do you call a
parade of rabbits
hopping backward?
A receding hare-line.

Why did the scarecrow
win an award?
Because he was outstanding in his field!

I'm on a seafood diet.
I see food, and I eat it.
I ♥ FOOD

Why did the
bicycle fall over?

Because it was
two-tired.

Did you hear about the restaurant on the moon?
Great food, no atmosphere.
LUNA BITES

I bought a belt made of watches.
It was a waist of time.

I was going to make a
joke about an elevator,
but it's an uplifting
experience.

What do you call a
fake noodle?
An impasta!
WANTED

Why don't skeletons fight each other?
They don't have the guts.
SKELETON SHOWDOWN
No guts... no glory!

SQUAWK!
What's orange and sounds like a parrot? A carrot.

Why did the coffee
file a police report?
It got mugged.

I once wrote a song
about a tortilla.
Well, actually it was more
of a wrap.

I used to play piano by ear, but now I use my hands.

What do you call cheese that isn't yours?

Nacho cheese.

I fell for an
electrician.
I was shocked.

I'm reading a book about
the history of glue.
I just can't put it down.

What do you call a
lazy kangaroo?
Pouch potato.

I told my doctor I broke my arm in two places. He told me to stop going to those places.

SALAD SPA
Why did
the tomato
turn red?
Because it saw the salad dressing!

Why did the music
teacher go to jail?
Because he got caught with
too many notes.

What do you call a
sleeping bull?
A bulldozer.

Why did the student eat his homework?
Because the teacher said it was a piece of cake.

What do you call a
bear with no teeth?
A gummy bear.

Why did the cookie go to the hospital?
Because it felt crummy.

What do you call a
pile of cats?
A meow-ntain.

Why did the man get fired from the orange juice factory?
He couldn't concentrate.
ORANGE JUICE FACTORY
FIRED

My friend got crushed
by a pile of books,
but he only has his
shelf to blame.

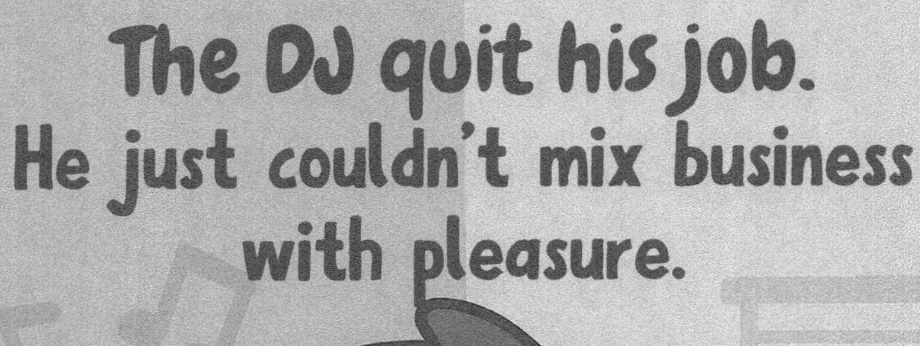

The DJ quit his job.
He just couldn't mix business
with pleasure.

I'm writing a book about reverse psychology.
Please don't read it.

What do you call a fish wearing a bowtie?
So-fish-ticated.
50TH UNDERSEA GALA

Why did the invisible man turn down the job offer? He couldn't see himself doing it.
We'd love to have you!
JOB OFFER

PIG DOJO
HOME OF THE PORK CHOP

What do you call a
factory that makes
good products?
A satis-factory.

I used to date
a baker.
She was a real cutie pie.

I used to be a
Velcro salesman,
but I couldn't stick with it.

I'm trying to organize a hide and seek contest, but good players are hard to find.
HIDE AND SEEK CONTEST

Why did the man get hit by a bike every day?
He was in a vicious cycle.
BIKE ROUTE DAILY!

I know a lot of jokes about retired people...
RETIRED HUMOR DEPT.
CLOSED TODAY
(and tomorrow)
But none of them work.

Why did the man get hit by a bike every day?
He was in a vicious cycle.
BIKE ROUTE DAILY!

I know a lot of jokes about retired people...
RETIRED HUMOR DEPT.
CLOSED TODAY
(and tomorrow)
Z Z Z
But none of them work.

What do you call a
sleeping dinosaur?
A dino-snore.

I used to work at a blanket factory,

but it folded.

I got a job at a
calendar factory,
but I got fired for taking
too many days off.

I used to be a banker,
but I lost interest.
0%
INTEREST
0%
INTEREST
BANK

I tried to be a tailor,
but I just didn't seam to fit in.

I couldn't figure out
why the baseball kept
getting bigger...
then it hit me.

I told my guitar it wasn't working.
It just stringed me along.

I once opened a gym
for ghosts,
but it didn't have much spirit.

I thought about
being a mime,
but I couldn't keep my
mouth shut.

BLAH BLAH

What do you get when
you cross a snowman
and a vampire?
Frostbite.

I would avoid the sushi if I were you. It's a little fishy.
TODAY'S SPECIAL:
TRUST ROLL
TRUST ROLL

I took a job as a
human cannonball.
BLAST
CAREER MOVE
It was the blast I needed.

I stayed up all night wondering where the sun went.
Then it dawned on me.

Why can't your nose be 12 inches long?
Because then it would be a foot.

I used to be addicted to the hokey pokey, but I turned myself around.

I walked into a lamppost yesterday.

It was enlightening.

I spilled herbs all over my keyboard.
Now it's thyme to reboot.
UGH...

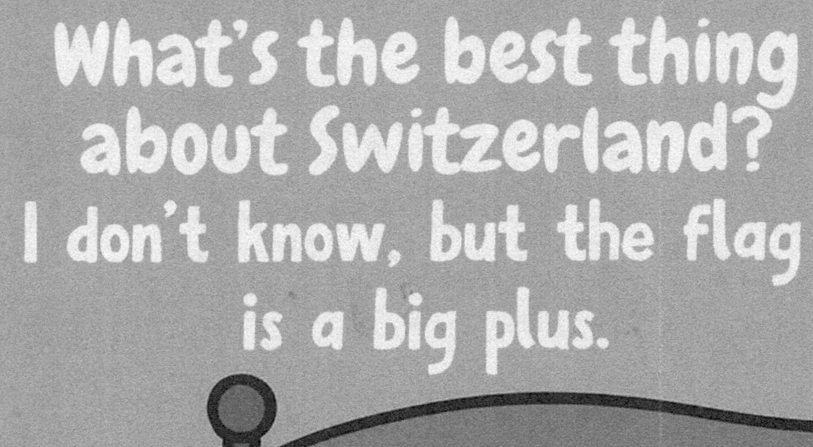

What's the best thing about Switzerland?
I don't know, but the flag is a big plus.

I got hit in the head
with a can of soda.
Good thing it was a soft drink.
PHEW!
SODA

Why don't eggs
tell jokes?
They'd crack each other up.
OPEN MIC
SHELL-SHOCKING
HUMOR

Why don't elephants use computers?
They're afraid of the mouse.

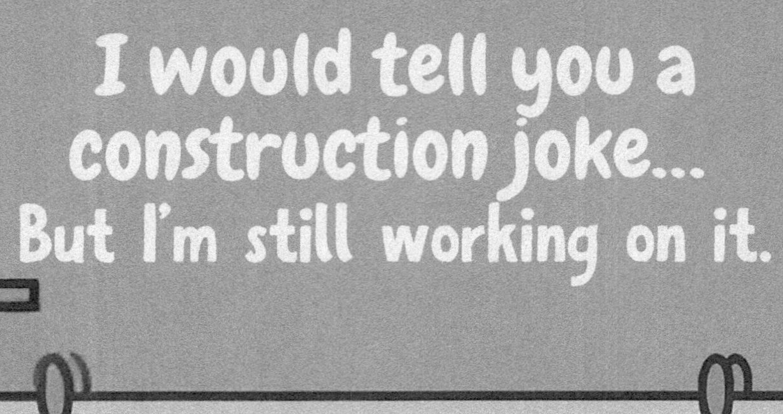
I would tell you a construction joke...
But I'm still working on it.
CONSTRUCTION JOKE—
UNDER CONSTRUCTION
PUNCHLINE

I tried to catch some
fog yesterday.

Mist.

I opened a bakery in space.
It's called
"Planet of the Crepes."

What do you call two
birds in love?
Tweethearts.

I considered becoming a chef,
I couldn't meat the expectations.

I once got into a fight at the airport.
It was terminal.
TERMINAL B
BOA DING PASS

What did one lightbulb
say to the other?
"I love you watts and watts."

Why did the chicken go to the seance?
To talk to the other side.
THEY'RE HERE!

I asked the librarian if the library had any books on paranoia.
She whispered, "They're right behind you."
MYSTERY
HORROR
STORIES
THRILLER

Why don't some couples
go to the gym?
Because some relationships
don't work out.

I told ten puns to my friends hoping one would make them laugh. No pun in ten did.
BORING

I only know 25 letters of the alphabet.
I don't know y.
ABCDEFGH
IJKLMNOP
QRSTUVWX
XZ

My friend said he didn't
understand cloning.
I said, "That makes
two of us."

Why don't oysters donate to charity? Because they're shellfish.
HELP SEA CREATURES

Why don't ducks ever grow up?
Because they quack under pressure.
HIGH

I used to hate facial hair... but then it grew on me.

Why was the
broom late?
It swept in.
Phew!

The shovel was a groundbreaking invention.

I was struggling to figure out how lightning works, but then it struck me.

I was going to tell you a joke about procrastination...
LATER
LATER
LATER
LATER
JOKES
A
But maybe later.

I used to be
indecisive.
Now I'm not sure.

What did the duck say when it bought lipstick?

"Put it on my bill."

I asked the librarian if they had any books on sarcasm.
She said, "Yeah, right."
SARCASM 101

I got a job at a bakery
because I
kneaded dough.

Geometry is just plane fun.

I gave all my batteries away.
They were free of charge.

Why don't graveyards ever get overcrowded? People are dying to get in.

I accidentally swallowed some food coloring.
The doctor says I'm okay but I feel like I've dyed a little inside.

What did the buffalo say
to his son when he left
for college?
Bison.